TWENTY SEVEN
STINGS

JULIE EMERSON

TWENTY SEVEN

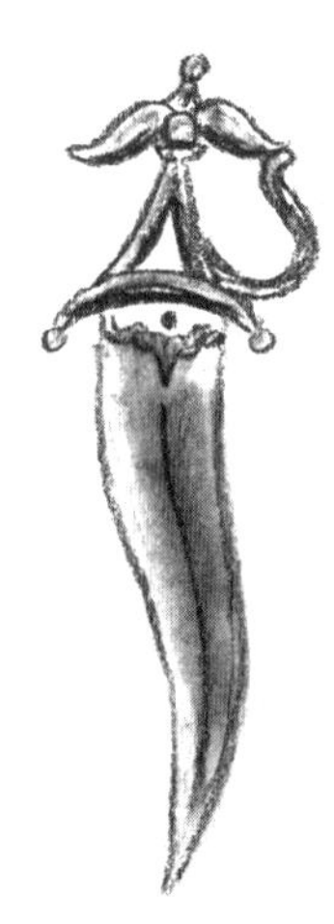

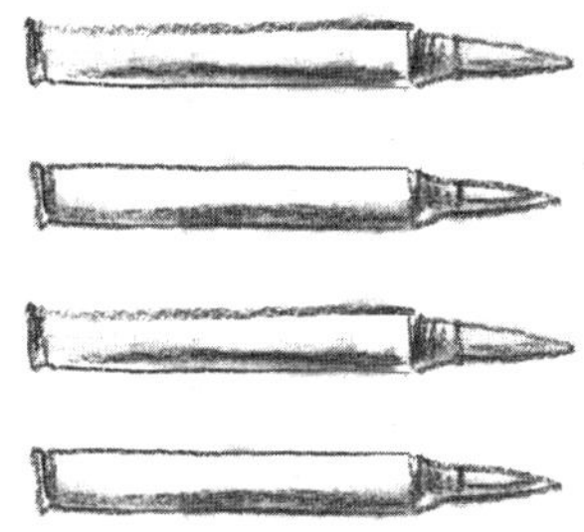

STINGS

ILLUSTRATED BY

ROXANNA BIKADOROFF

New Star Books
Vancouver
2015

Published by New Star Books Ltd.
www.NewStarBooks.com

CANADA
No. 107 – 3477 Commercial St.
Vancouver, BC
V5N 4E8

USA
No. 1517 – 1574 Gulf Rd.
Point Roberts, WA
98281

The publisher acknowledges the financial support of the Canada
Council for the Arts, the Government of Canada through the Canada
Book Fund, the British Columbia Arts Council, and the Government of
British Columbia through the Book Publishing Tax Credit.

Cataloguing information is available from Library and Archives
Canada, www.collectionscanada.gc.ca/

Illustration by Roxana Bikadoroff
Design by Oliver McPartlin
Printed and bound in Canada by Imprimerie Gauvin, Gatineau, QC.
First printing November 2015

TWENTY SEVEN STINGS

Contents

TWENTY SEVEN STINGS

The Island

c. 332 BCE (Tyre)

Observe the dog on the beach, splashing, chewing
snails, its mouth the story of purple dye.
The time is sunrise, dogstar Sirius rising
(so important, coins have stars or dogs.)
The slime from Murex snails would mark Tyre,
a sandspit island of urns of Tyrian purple;
to Pliny, dark but brilliant clotted blood.
For thousands of years, shells were crushed and boiled
Murex married an imported animal bride –
Bombyx, in violet that would never fade.
This silk, worth more than gold, Phoenicians traded
to royalty. Such wealth from the stench, the sea,
meant keeping books, thus the alphabet was made.

You are the tide, cajoling pebbles but failing
to breach the island's walls twice a day,
swatting ships for twelve years, frothing at the reefs
and only glimpsing the stinking rich pray
at Melkart's temple and sip from artesian wells.
So why the rocks ripped from the city dropped
in the sea, the wooden towers wrapped in leather,
the giant screen between them for Alexander
to hide the path he's building on the water
from the mainland, half a mile – stopped?
The fire ship: the Tyrians piled timber
and pitch on a ship, weighted it aft, towed it
to the causeway; cauldrons of oil on the masts
tipped and ignited the engineering project.

The luck of islands: Alexander, twenty,
assembles a navy, lobs stones at the walls
from catapults but divers slash his anchor
ropes; some sea monster bumps the causeway.
For Alexander, this man atop a tower,
arrows dart like dolphins through a gap.
Tyrians pour molten lead and huge
dishes of hot sand on the Macedonians.
Alexander leaves for a nap at two
every day, his enemies note and attack.
What destiny: this once, he comes back.
He defeats the islanders and completes the landfill.
Sold into slavery, thirty thousand people.
A catapult is dragged across to the temple
so Alexander can kneel there in a purple cloak.

The Walkers

c. 506 BCE (Wu, China)

i

I'll tell you how to walk, said Sun Tzu.
The king's women smiled at the master of war.
Walk to the right, he said. The ladies giggled.
Was I unclear, he asked. No, you
two leaders, walk to the left. They laughed.
If you laugh at me, he said, I'll kill you.
He did, and right away the rest obeyed.
The king cried and made Sun a general.

ii

To you it looks like we're doing nothing:
busy ants walking back and forth,
cleaning footware, packing tools,
walking together
>   *that's more than you can say for*
We trust each other. The knives are sharp, serrated;
we keep the sheaths spotless. Afterwards
our dreams are red
>   *you've never seen so much*

6

The toes are really not a part of us, such
little bits of flesh. When separated
from us, they're ridiculous. There's a ritual
but mistakes happen
                    under stress, you know
We're the walkers. Practice and discipline is all
we need. Our leaders had the bandaged toes,
took the shots, assumed the limp
with pride, suffered
                    you think I'm some insensitive
well someone has to do it, the common good.
It hurts to walk and we require
a tough hide
                    you can't imagine in a hundred
years later, you will not understand.

Marathon

c. August 12, 490 BCE (Greece)

i

Four days' wait. Now
barely light, lentils of water
on bay leaves. Some ships left
but the whole plain still seethes
with Persians and horses. I ask how
we can win; my slave says their shields
are wicker. I ask Athena for help;
my slave says gods may not exist.
He brings bread and figs and cheese.
My slave, the butter-eater from Thrace,
laughs with me at Persians gobbling
green nuts. Spartans are celebrating.
Our hero ran all the way
there and back but they won't fight.

Helmets and greaves on, we are a phalanx
running, shields covering the right,
in dense ranks of eight at the flanks,
arrows tapping bronze, we meet
men with long hair and nothing
but cloth vests, like women, I think,
the blade sinks, I pull it out,
plunge, veer to the centre, and beat
through bodies in pieces, bones
crack, organs spurt, groaning
barbarians fall bellowing in the swamp,
we roar the rest back to the sea,
plash in after and mob some boats.

ii

Trudging up from the beach, wet,
hoping not to hear much
more today, we must get
to Athens before the Persians sail
around the cape and attack. My slave
packs my armour, the flutes keep
time for the seven hours, running
on the flat, from the second hour it's slow
on the hills. He drops my spears in the fennel.
I yell at him for being old,
forty. He proffers a claypot of onions
and barley we eat with our fingers. No
fish. My slave says once the world
was water and men came from fish.
He took me to school every day
and this is something I didn't know.

My older sister has never been
to class, or a market. May she never
see men as I did. How
many goats sacrificed
for Persians killed? Let me rest
under an olive tree. No,
Athens will fall undefended,
my slave says, democracy destroyed.
We march, the road slopes down.
My slave whispers, rich men
will betray the city from within
if we let them. No loyalty.
He tugs grapes from vines for me,
almost ripe. We share some water.
They'll sack the harvest, my slave says,
and restore the tyrant. We can see the walls
of Athens. We are thousands strong, a force
that will push back the Persian fleet,
and I say to my slave, you are free.

Torched

330 BCE (Persepolis)

(Drunk courtesan leaping up,
girl musicians sliding from couches
of men crowned with laurel leaves,
men without trousers talking
philosophy, feasting the god of excess)

How much alcohol did
Thaïs raises a golden cup
to Alexander, whose cock conquered
the Persians, the Palace must be his.
The hundred-column hall: his,
the tributes of weapons and lions from Susa,
embroidery and horses from Babylonia,
treasuries of taxes and star charts,
prayers and epic poems: his.

(Ripping open a pomegranate, spraying
red dots across her breasts)

Just because some woman
To Alexander, first to see
Lammasu lions with men's heads
and eagle wings above the empire
of subjects celebrating spring.

Did we fear their stone soldiers?
Did we let them keep their silver?
Did their ancestors set fire
to Athens with no consequences?
(Grabbing torches, Thaïs and the girls
singing revenge and ready to burn
down the Palace for Dionysus)

All she had to do
Would a sovereign king
claim or destroy the enemy culture?
Would Alexander stagger
up the hundred eleven steps,
hurl his own blazing torch
at the Palace of limestone and cedar?
Would he reasonably regret the impulse
before he died at thirty-two?

postscript:
How many times has
The historian warned him: without me
you're nothing, and I won't bow.
It's written. Who cares how
the historian himself died. (Hanged)

Poison Maiden

c. 318 BCE (Pataliputra, India)

Sucking sugarcane,
the girl is crossing the moat,
passing pillars with silver
birds, entering the palace.

Think of the king, prone, massaged with rollers of ebony,
ringed by women archers, fed the professor's potion —
each day a drop of poison to foil the enemy.
The professor writes recipes for leprosy, fever
caused by powdered leech and jimsonweed and cow
dung mixed with mongoose tongue in a cobra's mouth.
Death took the queen at dinner, after one bite;
the prince was born fast with a blue spot on his brow.

The girl is still in ignorance
of the army's six branches:
soldiers, horses, elephants,
supplies and ships and chariots.

The professor burns frogs, testing toxic smoke
to aim at enemies, using every means to an end -
each day a drop of poison to bring immunity.
The people bet on dogs, he predicts the economy.
With sixty four gates to the city, how many
foreigners sneak in? A girl is intercepted.
A pale-skinned virgin with a tuneful walk, too
pale, unbound breasts, skin slightly blue.

The girl doesn't kill
insects, eat roots
or risk a Jain rebirth
in eight levels of hell.

From the country of Nanda, the girl is a gift to the king,
she tells the professor. Unaware, she must be,
each day a drop of poison was given to produce
a poison maiden: one kiss and the enemy
will die. He appreciates her waist, the irony.
He won't disturb the king, being fitted in the softest
cotton, and sends the girl to the elephant-riding Porus,
the tall ruler whose death will hand him the Valley

Barsine

c. 323 BCE (Susa, Greece)

I will remember
> before I became
>> a spoil of war.
My father was noble:
> he lost a battle
>> when I was seven.
Macedonians captured
> my beautiful mother,
>> my sister and brother
and me. My grandmother
> bowed to Alexander's
>> friend instead.
Alexander said
> they were one
>> and smiled. On the throne
his feet didn't reach
> the floor. His mother
>> slept with snakes.
He gave grandmother
> wool to weave
>> like some woman
in Greece, offending
> a Persian Queen;
>> he begged her pardon.

My father offered
         a ransom of land
                  and me as a bride.
Alexander declined
         since he could take
                  whatever he wanted.
Fairhaired, one
         blue eye, one brown,
                  taught by Aristotle.
Persian women,
         he said, are torments.
                  Then my mother
died in childbirth.
         We were studying Greek
                  in a Susa school.
I remember crying.
         I had no breasts.
                  I was betrothed to Mazaeus.
The girls laughed
         at Persian boys
                  wearing pants.
My father was strong:
         once he forced
                  a treacherous eunuch
to drink the poison
         meant to kill him.
                  He had scythed chariots.

His applebearers
        in felted caps
                and fishtailed mail
held a spear
        with a golden apple
                as counterweight.
In September Mazæus'
        horsemen torched
                the fields, thatched
roofs burned, black
        smoke enshrouded
                a red moon.
Fate blew
        a wind from the west,
                the moon went
dark as lapis:
        the eclipse foretold
                the end of the era.
We were taught the Greek
        battlecry *alalai*.
                My father would die
after he fled,
        wheels entangled
                in dead bodies,
escaping on horseback
        for eleven days,
                slain by his embittered

left wing general,
    pursued but not killed
        by my future husband.
King of Kings,
    Alexander wore
        white and purple
Persian robes.
    My grandmother
        he called mother.
The girls at school
    told stories
        about Alexander's body:
so sweet-smelling.
    They spoke of Babylon,
        the hanging gardens,
the road for Alexander
    carpeted with flowers
        and altars of perfumes.
There were lions and leopards.
    Mazaeus surrendered
        there, he became
a loyal governor
    until he died
        when I was twelve.
Who would imagine
    my wedding at sixteen,
        with ten thousand

Greeks marrying

    Persian women

        at the Susa Palace,

a five-day feast,

    a purple, scarlet

        and gold carpet.

Alexander called

    me Stateira,

        the name of my mother.

My sister married

    his best friend.

        The two men

loved each other

    more than anyone.

        I lived in the harem.

I drew triangles,

    I ate dates

        and saffron cream.

Alexander dreamed

    of harmony among nations.

        He trained Persians

with Greek weapons;

    they kissed him hello;

        his own men objected.

He was drinking so

    much, all night,

        and passing out.

Why his friend
        didn't wake up
                agonized him, then
he had malaria,
        they said, in Babylon,
                and died.
A widow in a year.
        In a week grandmother
                starved herself.
His old wife,
        pregnant too,
                sent me fruit.
I've eaten a melon,
        my belly is in spasms.
                my hands are numb.
The unsung wife
        of Alexander,
                I wanted
my life.

Truceless – The Mercenary War

c. 240 BCE (Carthage)

i

So you don't drink.
The liver, the sugar, the ticker,
it's not the capability.
Choose a girl companion
for the businessmen's dinner.
We pay, she's young and pretty,
she'll drink and she's the one
who'll get drunk and pass
out; her job is done.
Right away we replace
the girl, and we keep going.
No, they're making money
and you save face.
We're the men, running
the show, negotiating
the spoils of the earth. Refuse
to sit at the table, you lose
the chance to not be a slave.

ii

Eighty one tons of silver
surrendered to Rome got the soldiers
out of Sicily back to Carthage.
Mercenaries made war, the cost
of dead horses and corn rations
went up with soldiers' unpaid wages.
Glorious Carthage gave excuses
along with game and strong wine
to tens of thousands of mercenaries,
with their wives, idle, demanding more.
Promises to Celts during the war,
promises from Senators afterwards:
not enough. Food and taxes
from Libya fueled Carthage's exploits.
A Libyan facing reprisals, a reckless
runaway slave incited rebellion.
All the women tore off their necklaces
and gold rings to finance the fight.

iii

Gimel means throw a stick,
kill him. Don't think
of torturing prisoners? *Gimel,*
the Gaul says, get it?
Don't understand the others?
They're all from elsewhere:
where Hercules smashed
a strait through the pillars,
where Celts leave gifts
for rivers, Majorca – where
toddlers become slingers,
Hispania – where tusked
hyraxes crawl up rocks.
Translate the leaders' rant
a dozen ways, they're drunk,
Gimel you understand.
The job pushes discipline
underwater and drowns it. *Gimel.*

iv

A hundred and ten elephants in Utica
routed the rebels, their carnival infantry
of Iberians in purple-edged tunics,
Libyans with spears and Numidian cavalry.
Hanno captured their camp and baggage,
satisfied, left for dinner in the city.
The mercenaries, with seven years'
experience in Sicily, saluted the hasty
departure, attacked and took control.
All will go: Hanno, the navy,
the soldiers. A fearless Numidian dropped
his javelin, defected, and married the daughter
of the general. The mercenaries' policy:
keep to high ground, avoid
the elephants. But they ate each other,
starting with captives and slaves, when trapped
in the Valley of the Saw without food.
Remaining rebels were slaughtered by elephants.

Horses

c. 208 BCE (Mongolia)

Do exactly what I tell you; obey
me, said his father. Modu did.
When he was stronger, his father sent him away
from home as a hostage. Modu came back
on a stolen horse and got ten thousand
mounted archers along the Yellow River.

Do exactly what I tell you; obey
me, said Modu. He shot his favourite horse
and those who didn't follow lost their heads.
From far away he saw his lover sweep
her hat off, lift her hair from her neck. Modu
drew his whistling arrow; his men did, too.

Do exactly what I tell you, he said.
Modu aimed at his father's horse – no
archer hesitated. No historian
can guess why the old man said yes
to the son's next hunting trip. Family
lost to loyalty of Modu's ten thousand
men following orders. Modu's arrow
pierced his father's chest, then came the rest:
his brother, his stepmother – after killing
them all, the orphan psychopath was chief.

My horse, Modu said, in the Gobi desert,
is coveted by the king of Donghu. Modu sent
the horse to him. Weakness, thought his men.
My consort, Modu said, is desired by the king.
She's the one who smells of peaches. Pretty
cheeks wet with tears, she was sent.
Why would he give her up, thought his men.
My land, Modu said, is wanted by the king.
A thousand li of sand— not worth
our whistling arrows, thought his men.

Do exactly what I tell you, said Modu.
Do not let my land go or you
will die. At daybreak, attack the Donghu.
The enemy doesn't know that I am stronger.
Before you slit his throat, tell the king:
wherever I say my home is, you can't
have it. Horses and humans don't count.

31

Twenty Seven Stings

c. 77 CE (Rome)

Dancers zoom in, it's dim and busy
on pulsing tiles, a glut of pussy willows
on hexes, girls in gravity boots veering
over – former maids and greeters who gave
away sweet perfume – shrugging bitty
wings and fizzing antennae – this close
to leaving, if they figure out the wiggling
hips. This trip will be beyond the roses.
But first a stint at the door accepting bribes
from intruders, drop in the basket please. Zipping
out now, dozens of bees in blazing sun.

Jolt.

Dark in a jar.

Crammed tight, stoppered, where's mother?
Five eyes blinded, scared silly.
Headed for a scarecrow as a war bonnet
or flung at enemies from the edge of a parapet
or loaded, unbeknownst, on a catapult.
The urn is buzzing, cracked apart, bananas –
bees' alarm scent spreads. Screams as
barbed stingers pierce soldiers' flesh.
Every girl dies, her tiny belly
aloft with pollen, ripped off with the stinger.
How many of these venomous girls to kill
a man? Twenty seven, said Pliny.
From architecture to chaos, honey, I'm home
will not survive, and that will win the battle.

Straw Men

c. 756 (Yongqiu, China)

No food, no weapons, we had nothing but straw;
countless rebel soldiers were climbing the wall.
We lit the straw bales on the edge and pushed them
over; men fell in flames, there was a smell
of grilled meat. In the fields we caught sparrows
and rats to eat. General Zhang said dummies,
but boys could not craft something out of nothing,
so women rolled a thousand men from straw,
trimmed the torsos, plumped the bellies,
tied sticks between the legs, cinched heads,
made thick twitchy arms. We had no arrows.
We leashed the thousand and waited in our beds.
In the dark the dummies were lowered down the gate
and soldiers shot them. We pulled out bloodless

arrows, armed our men, and boiled weeds.
General Zhang said warriors, eat, and later
tonight, slip down. This second time the soldiers
smirked so we ran over and set their tents
on fire. We cooked our rice with shredded paper
and then we ate the horses. The next battle,
we ate bark. We didn't have the power
to fight back. One woman was precious.
General Zhang said concubine, come here.
She was fat and lazy — that was fatal.
Every bit of her was shared amongst us;
we chewed our dinner and didn't wonder who
comes next, for who had offered her and saved us?
No straw man, our hero General Zhang.

Nzinga

c. 1656 (southern Africa)

Think of Nzinga, refusing to stand
for the seated Portuguese governor –
using a kneeling slave as a chair.
The bishop sits on marble, baptizes
the captured in boatloads rowed
to slave ships in port; the red
sandstone cliffs spice the fog.
Nzinga, bow and arrows in hand,
a sword, an ax, and bells of iron,
holds a Christian name in reserve.
The Ngola hunter's power is the red
heat of the blacksmith's forge.
Nzinga eliminates anyone
else in line: nephew, brother.
Nzinga's sign of war is the red
feather flicked through a nostril.

Get your slaves here: in a market,
a battle, a tribute. For some, asylum
arranged by Nzinga, who deals with all
but the puppet king, and escapes east.
Nzinga, with the Jaga, cuts off
the heads of humans and drinks their blood.
Red tacula trees in the rain
sweat eight months a year.
Nzinga keeps sixty lovers.
Red flames slap the cassava
pot dashed with water in a calabash.
Portuguese drown Nzinga's sister.
To the Dutch, in their turn at the Trade,
Nzinga sells prisoners of war.

Bisimbi, the dead, live with us.
Bush vipers kill and adapt
to survive, changing from green to red.
All our infants must die,
Nzinga orders, the sons of slain
enemies trained as expendable soldiers.
Nzinga's other sister Barbara
is alive, captive for eight years.
With Brazilians in power, Nzinga
exchanges for Barbara: trade fairs,
a hundred backs with red lashings,
a Christian mission — and infanticide
must end. The family line
is drawn in the red blood of women,
a matrilineal clan. Nzinga
the warrior is not a man. Say it,
Nzinga is a woman leader,
say, a woman leader is Nzinga.

Divine Winds

August, 1281 (Kyushu, Japan)

Humps of a green dragon in Hakata Bay:
the islands were easy to take. We said, submit
to Khublai the father, benevolent ruler.
A Christian mother and Buddhist wife meant
mercy. We had grenades, masses of arrows,
and Mongol horses; from our forges, smoke rose
straight up from four thousand ships.
And all along the coast a miserable wall.
We dreamed of the Cane Palace, huge and gilt,
disassembled every August and rebuilt.

They waited with white pennants; little waves.
We held back our drums and cavalry, and fire
bombed the harbour, recalled the seige of Ghengis:
his ordering ten thousand swallows, tying
firecrackers to their tails, the birds flying
back to burn their cities. The wind blew,
the pines went black. Pirates and Samurai
climbed aboard, carapaced in leather
scales of many layers laced together.
Each stranger yelled a name and rank.

Killing was work. Women were hung from the bow,
their hands pierced and roped, red drops
sluiced into whitecaps. We chained the ships.
For seven years, the Japanese had cut off
our envoys' heads and prepared for an attack.
The sea rolled. We called our fighters back
from the hills behind the wall. Crammed, wet,
in the sleeping decks, it smelled of camphor, sweat,
cedar caulked with tung oil, and men imagining
the hundred Mongol girls in Khublai's harem.

No war cries. The west wind slammed
against us, waves lifted ships jammed
together, fir masts toppling, cracking
in pieces, we were sinking and couldn't head out.
The dragons' eyes on the prow couldn't see
the typhoon coming. All was white foam,
as white as Khublai's hundred thousand horses.
I rode a plank, one of the few fated
to live. They caught and chained me the next day,
walking on timber and corpses across the bay.

1914 /1916

(Europe & America)

1914

Standing in a grave in a field, we shored it up,
took tea and biscuits, artillery
shuddered, blood music, we fired a mortar
toffee apple through barbed wire. Water
to our knees, the ratsfoot, we just clamber
over, targets in helmets, glassnecks
break, boys eating dirtcake.
Spades are gravespoons for the lifecrackers.
A truce so all the boys can come shyly
out on the dance floor to bury the dead.
Raid: killed a German in his mudbed.
We have whiteseeping wounds, hot licefingers,
the skyblister hits, firewashes
our eyelashes, cooks hair, our heads
get the gas opera, the godletter.

1916

Wilson kept them out of war (aside
from six invasions south), pacifists clutter
the streets, so he won. America is neutral,
selling steel and fuel to both sides.
Wilson pitches freedom for other countries
combined with military intervention.
Crusaders and Saracens: not careful
discrimination of German immigrant from Hun.
Culture is crucial: in films, after Belgium,
Germans cross the ocean to attack, books
by Germans are burned, photos of fallen soldiers
aren't allowed. Sabotage and Sedition
will jail war protesters, Wilson will make
the world safe for democracy, it will take
years of Uncle Sam pointing at you.

Big Men

c. 1940 (Europe)

45

Starvation is a weapon, said the Big Men.
That was when a Polish child would hunt
potatoes and a Dutch child would suck a beet.

Submit to famine the ordinary German
and starve the towns they occupy so families
throw off the yoke of Hitler, wrote Churchill.
That was when a French child smashed a chair
before a meal to burn its legs for heat.

Hundreds of millions of eggs were rolling over
borders. The plan was, the top German caste
would never be hungry again: tons of wheat
diverted, other people eat last.
Slash the workers' protein, calculate
percents below the minimum to implement
racial feeding, reduce the rations for Jews
to zero. Cattle and people would compete
for fodder; the fat of the land to the master.
That was when a Jewish child could have
no eggs, no fruit, no vegetables, no fish, no meat.

Sledges of vegetables came on the frozen lake
to Leningrad, after warehouses of food
were bombed first: a city under siege.
But a third of the people starved; the aim was achieved.
That was when a Russian child would take
a zoo animal or boil a wallet to eat.

Bulging sacks of flour had sifted through
the portholes of ships, sailing past the blockade
by Churchill in the first war - food for Belgians,
approved by sympathetic Americans as aid
for stricken souls, not for empty stomachs.

Subhumans, stated Hitler, should be destroyed.
So that was his intention; was it inaction
by Churchill, rather, when beastly people starved
in Bengal? The war would cut imported rice,
officials and a cyclone stripped more. The famine
could be helped if he accepted offers
of foodstocks for India, he kept them back.
Millions perish. A child dies.

Misdirection

c. 1944 (England)

Bigbobs off the English coast:
floating canvas landing crafts,
plywood artillery, and inflated rubber
tanks looked real to Germans in the air.
Expecting camps for an attack at Calais,
they saw kitchens – telltale smoke
from chimneys three times a day,
Operations Quicksilver and Cabbage.
They heard a life thick and luscious
with noise: orders, shooting practice,
the fracas of assault rehearsals, the clamour
of embarkations, planned invasions.
Women sent the wireless transmissions
(in cipher) – all faked. The glory of war,
General Sherman said, is moonshine.
Then British pilots sent bogus
radio signals: *moonshine,*

dropped paper tinsel to black
out screens: *window*. Seen through,
a fleet of ships appeared below.
Balloons at three heights reflecting
looked like five thousand tons
sailing towards them. Filling in the blanks.
Reconnaissance over Norway drew
attention from Normandy, the English knew
(from secret codes). Turing questioned
how close a computer could be
to a man, he cracked Enigma, with others.
Every message revealed. Who
could conceive of sixty million deaths?
Turing was indecently close to a man
so his government castrated him.
He killed himself after the war.

water, fire, wood, earth, air

August, 1346 (Crécy, France)

water

what is water but provocation:

crossing on split oak and a main sail, rushing

bridges, rebuilding ones wrecked to stop us razing

their towns, we are not just an island nation,

wading the river to Caen, at low tide fording

the mouth of the Somme, to set up Edward to beat his cousin,

after the famines from the wet summers, eating and drinking

French wine, yeomen ready when it started raining

before the battle, our bowstrings tucked in

our cloaks, then thick as snow our arrows covering

the Genoese at the front, their crossbow strings loose and sodden.

fire

so beautiful we burned them down:

abbeys, bridges, castles, cathedrals, a whole town.

A riot of pillaging, we reduced their wealth to force a fight.

Our royal kitchen had purveyors of poultry, buttery, scullery,

apothecary, bakery, spice, fish and flesh, and for the rest

of us, sumptuary regulations and no meat.

Excessively buttoned clothes were evidence of moral laxity.

Our Black Prince had a suit of armor at eight, and a tent;

at sixteen he led us against the Oriflamme, red

for cruelty, victors give no quarter, our camp was lit

with great fires and torches and candles on Saturday night.

wood

for the king in a windmill on the hill:
a perfect site, before him the theatre, behind him the woods.
Our longbows were yew, wood from churchyard trees,
straight-grained without windshake, galls, or knots,
the belly heartwood, the backside sapwood, goosefeathers
on arrows tipped with barbed broadheads or quartered points.
Six a minute we shot, after yells and flutes
from crossbowmen who left their wooden shields in their carts,
falling, retreating, too slow to load, so their nobles
advanced in ragged order to kill them — summer is for wars,
our curved fingers were callused from year-round practice.

   earth

dirt geometry clinches destiny:

the three divisions, parallel lines, the slope of the *V*

of longbowmen seated on the ground on down to flat farmland

between the road and the river, the dots of French cavalry,

five-point quincunx asterisk for our infantry,

four-spike caltrops to pierce enemy boots.

Knights dashed their horses into the heap, couldn't see

with sun in their eyes, dropped into ditches, our long knives

worked and our spades made massive trenches to bury

them. Soon the Black Death would pile bodies in the earth,

taking the tenant farmers and leaving the landowners with no family.

air

why does breath disappear:
only in a ray of light do we see the motes in the air.
The blind king of Bohemia, desiring a day of battle,
tied the reins of his horse to those of his men at each side;
the three died. His crest was three ostrich feathers.
Some men lost on their way to war slept in the fields.
Sunday morning, the scenery costumed in fog, there –
stolen Oriflamme standards drew the French over –
thousands more were murdered in the fog.
Called a coward, Edward vowed to conquer, on a dare,
took the vow of the heron and started the Hundred Years' War.

Fire

c. 200 BCE – 2012 (China – America)

55

Fire grabs green bamboo:
bam. Saltpeter is stuffed in
crates of firecrackers so the boom
scares evil spirits - sudden
entropy scatters disordered bits.
Bamboo won't open like a rose
unfurls or azalea buds awake,
striking us so with beauty,
its hot gas sizzles and explodes.
Hitch the fire to arrows, make
paper ground rats scurry
and enemies afraid. Lion heads
on Greek ships shoot flame,
Chinese soldiers' wooden dragons
are filled with gunpowder, the same
elixir in a fire lance or arquebus.

With fire, a man faces the enemy.
It's fear he offers, no screen
of scarlet tulips. A samurai's
sword compels the foe to face
the man, the knight with a spiked mace,
no blooming allium bulb.
The crossbowman can rupture
class, accused of cowardice
for not getting close to his rival.
Militiamen throng the fields,

muskets firing, nothing natural
as hundreds of blazing hawthorne buds.
Poppies turn blood-red,
pilots fly their own fire.
Now, beside a potted geranium
at his desk, a man with a screen is god.
He steers a dragonfly in another
country he's never seen, a mother
calls her teenaged son – the end,
unmanned. Songs efface the boom:
bam.

Frequently Asked Questions

Why did you write poetry about people making war throughout history?

I have always been a pacifist, and I wanted to understand war. Any benefits of understanding are dedicated to my creative collaborators, and to the hive of bees on the roof of my Main St. Studio.

How have bees and poisons been used in warfare?

In *Natural History*, completed in 77 AD, Pliny wrote that twenty-seven is the number of bee-stings required to kill an enemy. The wonderful graphic novel *Clan Apis* (2000) by Jay Hosler is about the lives of bees. *Greek Fire, Poison Arrows And Scorpion Bombs: Biological and Chemical Warfare in the Ancient World* (2003) by Adrienne Mayor details the way bees and toxins have been deliberately employed. She also described mithridatism, i.e. eating small amounts of poison in order to become immune to it while remaining (in legend) a deadly carrier.

What rules and philosophies of war have been written by men sitting inside?

Sun Tzu wrote about Chinese military strategy in *The Art of* War in the 6th century BCE, as did Sun Hai Chen in the more recent *The Wiles of War: 36 Military Strategies from Ancient China* (1991).

Chanakya (a.k.a Kautilya) was the advisor to the 4th century BCE Mauryan empire, and wrote the book on statecraft; he is considered the Father of Economics and the Indian Machiavelli.

Chroniques by Froissart is a sympathetic analysis (or openly biased account) of war in the 14th century between England and France, including the Battle of CrŽcy. The map of this battlefield, drawn by Hillaire Belloc in 1912, illuminates how landscape determines the rules of military strategy.

In *On War* (1832), Carl von Clausewitz wrote on European military thought; in *The Lesser Evil: Political Ethics in an Age of Terror* (2004), Michael Ignatieff writes on the weakness of the strong and the strength of the weak in present-day international conflict.

Game theory has analyzed the rule "The enemy of my enemy is my friend," (and the reverse), and this has been used to diagram positive and negative interactions among three or more nations.

What does it feel like to be on a Mongolian warship?

Step aboard the St. Roch, the Canadian icebreaker ship docked in the Vancouver Maritime Museum. From the 1940s, this boat sailed the Northwest Passage, and it is surprisingly similar in materials and dimensions to Mongolian boats of more than 700 years ago.

How did government propaganda tactics on civilians arise in the 20th century, and how did soldiers deal with their war experience?

The Great War of Words (1987) by Peter Buitenhuis explains the development of propaganda with the participation of North America in the European war of 1914-1918. Chris Hedges' *War is a Force that Gives Us Meaning* (2003) also deals with the emotions of the warrior.

According to reliable sources, or to snakes-with-wings sources, what happened in classical warfare?

Dip into *The Histories* by Herodotus (written in the 5th century BCE) and *The Histories* by Polybius (written in the 2nd century BCE). Plutarch, born in 46 CE, wrote *Life of Alexander.*

What are the ethics of using drones?

P.W. Singer has written *Wired for War – The Robotics Revolution and 21st Century Conflicts* (2009) and "The Ethics of Killer Applications: Why Is It So Hard to Talk About Morality When It Comes to New Military Technology?" (2010)

What is the short (but seemingly endless) poetic form of _Barsine?_

This is a triadic stepped line, three phrases with falling intonation, in the music of a casual sentence. William Carlos Williams used it in "Asphodel, That Greeny Flower" (1955).

What was it like to live as a pacifist or a soldier in the first world war?

The most illuminating British civilian novel written during the first world war is _Non-Combatants and Others_ by Rose Macauley (1916); the best British soldier's account may be Robert Graves's _Good-bye to All That_ (1929).

How did people implement plans to starve their neighbours to death in wartime?

Human Smoke: The Beginnings of WWII, The End of Civilization (2008) is a chronological collage of facts by the novelist Nicholson Baker. _Starvation Over Europe: Geopolitics of Hunger_ was written by Boris Shub and Zorach Warhaftig in 1943. _Letters to Freya: 1939-1945_ (1990) is a war narrative in letters by (my distant relative) Helmut James Graf von Moltke. As a Kreisau anti-Nazi resistance intelligence officer, he wrote the letters (which were hidden in a beehive) to his wife Freya, before he was executed.